I OWN NOTHING AND I BELONG NOWHERE

Alivia Francis

Dream Boy Book Club

ISBN: 979-8-9920663-0-2
Catalog Number: DBBC012

Dream Boy Book Club
dreamboybook.club
USA

Table of Contents

2 A.M.

I sit like a begging dog,
listening to drug-induced conversations,
wondering what is to come.
Maybe I'll go home and think,
"oh god, my own memories—
oh god, my own life!"
And so what?
I am inconsolable and I am tired.
I am blessed with being a woman.
I am scorned for being a woman.
I am forsaken to be heard
more so than to be seen.
I will speak before spoken to.
I will yell in the streets.
I will yell in the pub!
I will lay nude at the foot of the bed
and beg for forgiveness.

Haiku #1

I'd extend my arm
so far I'd break it if it
was to hold your hand.

So be it, I am drunk

I am an angel when I wake at four in the morning

but a devil to those who have never seen me at four in the morning.

I can feel how hard I am breathing,

I wonder if anyone questions my wellbeing.

I've been eating apples with jam and calling myself French,

the French would be disgusted by me if they knew me deeply.

I wonder how well the girl with the braids knows the man she is sitting next to at the bar...

They exchange words but it never feels like a conversation.

This reminds me that last night I dreamt of strangers

loving me like a mother would.

Overthinking after public speaking

"How extraordinary!"

No one felt the same.

In fact, we were all quite empty.

So to spare myself a return to the hospital—I saddled in for the night.

But I'll still claw at my brain while gently folding my laundry;

an immature individual leading a functional life, so-to-speak.

I fight with myself in the satin fabric section of the craft store before picking out bedsheets.

I've figured out how to sleep through the night

but I now choose to stay awake until dawn for selfish purposes.

I've always enjoyed a good meal—almost as much as I enjoy a run down a hillside,

but this doesn't mean much.

Hungover in New Orleans

I am utterly overflowing with emotions on this Monday morning.

Be it one too many long nights, or be it that I've got a soft heart.

But I am utterly overflowing with emotions.

The fifty-something year old across the street could blow her cigarette ash in my face and I would not forsake her for it—no.

I would understand her more.

I think if my mother called me at this moment I would have to decline,

no parent should know how deeply her daughter feels emotions.

And viewing life from this park bench entices you to see that most people are always moving,

but it's getting somewhere that's not so much.

Am I getting somewhere?

Unpleasant

I am joking, of course.
I was pathetic—
and I did suffer!
But these are all agreeable things.
For example,
I tried not to look offended.
Finding pleasure in a stubbed toe.
But anger...that is not so agreeable.
It pulls on my limbs,
anchors me to the floor.
"Ungrateful!" I'd hear,
"Lies!"
And maybe so!
But what was to be done?
I was hopeless...
hopeless and grotesque.
Begging for ecstasy
and ignoring profound ideals.

The wretched debriefing

Looking out the window, I feel myself—our bodies.
Summer has nearly begun, and summer is nearly
over.
A kiss, more sex.
He makes the bed how he used to as a child.
Can you climb inside of my ear and hear my brain?
He tells me,
"The music that gathers us, it will pass,
but it is up to us to continue tradition
or forsake it just as so."
It is noon and I have been left unprotected.
I say,
"Just because we have been wretched,
that does not mean we have not also been lovely."
So, here—in my house, the dog has run off
and I am asking to be forgiven.

This life

Normalcy was never a ripe apple hanging from a tree where I grew up.

Rather,

it was pennies and nickels to be found in between my parents' couch cushions.

"Have a cigar," never was a common term.

Unbroken, unshaven men had dawned the doors to heaven before I found out it did not exist.

And once more for the highway—once more for my baby,

who was working overtime on the road to the wishing well.

To whom it may concern

The person who said it is easier to ask for forgiveness than for permission has never looked up from the floor on both knees,

blinded with tears and remorse,

and asked someone they love to see past their demented mind

and look only at the remorse,

the intention,

the pain.

To look at them like they are God—pray to them,

bleed for them.

Begging to be wiped free of sin,

begging to be wiped free of the pain that brought me here.

For a moment we knew each other

There's an elderly woman on a reclining beach chair
with whom I take great pleasure in observing.

Though, I'd never speak a word of it.

It sets off a familiar feeling of observing a grandparent: I
watch her rise to water her lawn, wizened from the sun,
just as she has come to with age.

Occasionally, I witness her watching me.

I type on a computer that—in a much different way, is
aging me.

Gulping coffee in thirty-minute increments, knowing
that at any moment one of us will ultimately leave and
that will be it.

These brief looks towards a stranger will not be remem-
bered tomorrow.

In fact, we will be departing with even less than what we
entered with.

Yet, for these few simple but significant moments

where I'd glance upon someone so worn with the years
of watering a lawn,

it's as though that's all she's ever done for 80-some-odd
years.

And as for me,

to her I am always a face gazing upon a dirty computer
screen.

Drifting

May the rearview mirror never catch up to your last puff of smoke

and the shrewd winds never be passive enough to carry along the scent.

If anything is to be appreciated,

it most likely will be the conversations far and few between in the mornings,

and even so late at night.

Irony

The thought, intentional
but hanging like a wet rag in my hands.
Why have we swam across rivers
only to bathe in the sun?

The depressed person

In the way that felt dangerously shameful to admit—
thank you, thank you.
I have all too easily been the exact same since child-
hood.
Trying to get the gag in without getting scorned.
I would tell myself,
"The depressed person would dislike this,
would have not made any attempt to stay in touch."
It was while thinking this that I managed to mutter,
"Do you think anybody cares about us at all?"
All I heard back was a chuckle.

So we begin

Imagine it now: the howling protagonist.
Second by second—
every second is nakedly urgent!
Heuristic, but practiced only in secret.
As if hoping to discover something unspoken…
The blades of grass, dressed elegantly in dewdrops,
may make a song for those lingering on roadways.
Nothing will be remembered by daybreak.
So I look at you slowly, with tired and curious eyes,
"Pluck the petals off to see if we resemble the lily."

Insecurity, insecurity, insecurity

I did drown myself in your intelligence with no boat to bring me back to the shore.

And I did pour my soul into an empty glass and call it wine.

I've never had the sense of urgency for anything but love

or what I thought love was.

I've never intended to raise my voice nor silence myself.

So it goes,

the ending wrote itself as a fearful whisper in a game of telephone

and I had sworn myself to secrecy,

so our love died in silence.

We become what we say

There was a soft lingering that would last six weeks,

and it was true that, at this time,

I was not to be understood.

I had met you in a sheet of innocence,

disguising myself as a pretty little thing with a pinch of insanity,

corresponding with your intellect and sense of urgency.

That very spot is where we would learn

dependency goes hand-in-hand with impermanence.

The flawed self

Destined to be an observer,
to experience love feels sinful;
I reek of sin.
My lover can smell it on me
like a honeysuckle perfume.
Never to understand:
to hold me is to condemn me.

Feed me to your wolves

I felt it again this morning—the desire to be well.
Though, the same will come again tomorrow.
It's a common feeling, this beating in my chest,
but a rare one to a bartered heart.
Begging for blood and desire,
yet living solely on betrayal.

Haiku #2

Breaking my own heart
means staying where I've outgrown,
never feeling home.

There's no money in self-pity

I am unaware of what has become of me.

It aches and tickles my skin.

What beast has situated itself upon me?

What monster has lain at my feet?

I bathe in misfortune

and infatuation feeds on my angst.

True madness—that is the albatross around my neck.

I wake to pure chaos

witnessing the dog gnawing on my bones as if he had nothing more to eat.

But I think he was just sick of me too.

To remain delicate

Similar to tender words uttered through whispers:
Nights that feel calm also feel remarkable.

Longing, I know you

It's not just that my fingers find a way to move through the gaping holes of those that belong to another,

but the restless desire to trail them along skin not my own.

Perhaps this is a way of getting to know someone through touch alone.

It's intermittent:

Two hands fastening together for longer than a few subtle moments before they're back running over the inches that lay waiting to be unraveled.

This in itself is an exclamation of how deeply I know how to yearn without a word being said.

It's a dry ache that burns a wide mile.

Reality breeds cruelty

I observed a passionate man.
His hands,
teeth,
eyelids.
I observed a distracted mistress.
Destiny hath disappointed them both.

You and I and a bottle of wine

Deep and fleeting eye contact can—at will, devour
any two people inclined to be fed whole to the
heady power of infatuation.
Something which is more intoxicating than a bottle of
wine consumed by someone not yet accustomed to the
feeling of being drunk under the sun.
Squinting eyes beg to be seen as a reflecting image,
rather than a doorway.
Only made possible by the clouds above, lingering just
far enough away from the sun.
What they fail to realize:
the ability to fathom the existence of each other is only
made possible during the moments the clouds do not
remember to touch the sun.

To yearn is to live, to wait is to die

Sharing silence with strangers is a poetic sickness
and a violating affirmation of solitude.

Complying with unspoken cues:

There lies the way in which we speak through closed
mouths.

I no longer have a face

And I'm here again.

I am begging for people to miss me and I think,

who could miss someone who no longer has a face?

I've wiped mine clean after dirtying it day after day.

I've looked in the mirror and betrayed the person look-
ing back.

I look in the mirror...and now I no longer have a face.

I no longer have a face.

I no longer have a face.

To be together is to be alone

It's uncomfortably true that we're brilliant alone,

but lest we forget the importance of creating brilliance out of love.

To be selfless in the face of ourselves—to look into my own eyes and breathe a little more deeply...

Well,

there's not much to be learned after that

besides the art of letting go.

Which is nearly identical to the art of giving in.

I'm still in the house

Me,
the curtains,
my hips,
that fuzzy feeling in my stomach.
I didn't plan for this, so what is left?
Your broken beliefs, a good memory or two.
The mailman no longer comes either,
he didn't like my singing.
The birds nod to me on their journey north
and I still beg them to let me follow.
"Days are too short for your wingspan,"
blow some more hot air up my ass, I laugh.
I want the door always open,
it's easier for me to concentrate that way.
I take myself too seriously in refined spaces.

I'll be back in the morning

I was your playmate,
banished to be all that I ever could be.
A half-drunk bottle of wine that had been
left to grow old on your kitchen counter,
a bruise you watched heal.
My coat still waits by the door,
your feet hang off the bed.
I hoped you wouldn't notice,
would not sense the absence.
God, I begged for it!
Please don't notice.

Dissociating in front of people you love

My right shoe is always ahead of my left,

I was once told this is the first step towards independence.

Though, for me,

it seems to be the first step towards certain bad habits.

An indication that I was lacking brain cells and my pain receptors were put on autopilot.

"Not so present today are we?" he'd say,

all I could muster up was a grin.

Begging in the creases on your skin

I'm on my knees—primal.
I'm a mess.
Drawing breaths from screams;
bent like a tree branch
and flimsy in the wind of your breath,
wet from your drool.
Won't you whisper in my ear from above?
Show me the gentle feel of soft lips?
I need love that digs into my flesh.
To feel held, even from a distance.
So here, in your palms,
I find a way to still kiss your knuckles.

People watching

You lusted after it: balance.
Often I watched,
drawn in by the sense and nonsense
and the flying pieces of emotion.
"How very delicate..." I shrug it off.
What we need is the chaos of love
and the many tongues of poetry.

I will exist either way

You head home as I sit and watch,
pawing at my thoughts on my porch swing.
I am no longer being fed by a rich man,
and so I am free to live again.
I am free to starve.
I am free to sleep in a spare room on a stranger's futon
alone,
as I witness him show too much interest in me.
A bird may shit on my head during a long walk,
and a child may stare at me—confused.
All of this is true, and it means nothing.

Haiku #3

What must this passion
to yearn so explicitly
be but a virtue?

It sounded like the Pacific

When I was young and dumb
my lover said to me,
"I can hear the sea in a glass of wine."

Things grow in darkness

Introducing light to a cave

invites strangers to view secrets that previously were
hidden by fear;

but I've picked flowers from this dark cave

and these strangers never knew.

Fight or flight

Sunlight asks us to apprehend what is in front of us.

We fall victim to beauty without noticing its siren call.

And blind faith can feel like open arms to someone
with a flight response.

Haiku #4

Intermittently,
I care for myself so much
I forget to hurt.

The sunflower

I was a lady, it turns out.
Living in contemporary, adult life.
Making a home in the gray space
and burning my tongue on piping hot tea.
All the while,
conserving a flower within a book.
My silence.
His silence.
The sex.
The view from atop the stairs.
"How do you feel about empathy?"
Too much...too much.

Valderice

Sleepy hillsides

and grassy fields stand waiting—

calling me into a sea of wildflowers;

I am barefoot and listening quietly to the wind.

I don't mind the bumpy landscape,

I admire it.

Regret has no place here in the grass with me,

just the birds that land beneath the sunlight as I squint to see them.

For hours I gaze at soon-to-be memories,

all while producing a spot of shade for the bees below me.

And maybe this evening

honey will drop from my lips and onto yours,

but for now I am barefoot and listening quietly to the wind.

Haiku #5

I defile myself
by studying a face I'll
never see again.

Haiku #6

I'd barter my soul
for a heavenly exchange
of words between us.

Haiku #7

Goodnight darling, do
not forget to reflect on
what was lost in youth.

I am a heavy desire

My heart pours, bloody, into my palms.
Dripping from my fingers
like watermelon juice running down the rind.
Do you drool for a taste?
Or does the thought of sticky fingers
that comes with eating fruit with your bare hands
turn your face in disgust?

It's everywhere

There are women and men having sex in the apartment above mine.

There are two women next to me who look at eachother like they want to be having sex.

There are two men down the block who are texting their wives that they are out getting groceries but they are in a spare room having sex.

The doorman greets women in hopes that he can have sex.

The old lady who does my laundry dreams of having sex with her late husband.

The rats looking for scraps in the trash stop to have sex atop of an old salami bag.

The couple I passed going into the subway want to have sex so they can carry a child.

I'm sitting here in my bedroom and I want to be having sex.

And

And so I'll hold my right hand on my cheek—near the side, so my fingers will brush over my ear just like yours do.

And I'll laugh and paint the walls with my voice—my aching voice, because I didn't know I could be so loud, so happy.

And I feel so much passion in love that—at times, I too ache.

And I read over your poetic words that touch me just as deeply as your skin, I feel held.

And suddenly I'm the same age my mother was.

And I feel an overwhelming sense of warmth rush over my body when I hear your name.

Playing the numbers

Quietly,

before the mist rolls in—the people here are impeccably disguised,

like actors shouting over a couple of palm trees.

They wrap themselves in void.

Just as anybody would, they cry and shake for difficult love that is buried beneath soil,

but they also feel brilliant—confident, even.

Like someone always losing yet playing to win.

Thoughts when visiting

I feel seen by the man driving a grocery store mobile cart across a highway intersection.

I wear my mother's socks when I visit, they are always the low cut ones and I always accidentally take them home with me.

I've stifled myself again under the bliss of my own discretion.

Let the lights stay dim

My needy practice to be seen only through candlelight
is a pressing matter,

I never allow a flame to be blown out.

Thus creating a hefty amount of smoke inhalation,

warping my body into a paper mache parcel of what it
could have been

if I'd only bent over my bedside table to blow the candle
out.

Haiku #8

I could burn in your
arms with such passion that you'd
forget you're on fire.

Haiku #9

This feeling is far
too pensive, I'll wallow in
it a little more.

A dream I once had

They danced a little awkward...
turning,
crisscrossing,
a long, slow slide.
She is throwing up her hands
and he edges himself aside.
There they are, in a memory.

Come back to bed

Built up in iridescent lighting

like dust,

revealing what once rested here in place of my body.

I hold heat like an object in my arms: warm and dented

precisely in place of my own radiant skin.

But the brilliant hues—they never seem to remain for
more than the few seconds that they're revealed,

and why should they?

For a feeling is merely the moment that lies beneath it.

But we hold onto moments

and we make sweet melodies from how we remember
the shades of our eyes looking

when we are no longer in view of one another.